Dedication

To the Potential Digital Nomads,

This book is dedicated to you—the dreamers, the adventurers, and the seekers of a life less ordinary. May the pages that follow be a guiding light on your path towards embracing the digital nomad lifestyle and unlocking the world of endless possibilities that awaits you.

"Embrace the freedom to roam, for within the vast tapestry of this world lie the treasures of your wildest dreams. Let the winds of wanderlust carry you to distant shores, and in the embrace of new horizons, discover the magic that lies within."

With boundless optimism and unwavering belief in your potential, I invite you to step forward, embrace the unknown, and embark on a journey that will forever shape your soul. May your nomadic spirit find solace in the wise woman's words and lead you to a life filled with fulfillment, adventure, and the unwavering pursuit of your passions.

Safe travels and may your nomadic journey be an extraordinary one.

Jane-Ann Koci

CONTENTS

Foreword

Greetings, dear readers,

As I embark on this journey of sharing my experiences and insights as a digital nomad, I am filled with a sense of joy and gratitude. My name is Jane-Ann Koci, and as a Gypsy by heritage, the wanderlust flows through my veins, intertwining with my deep connection to the great outdoors. The call of exploration and the yearning for freedom are second nature to me, and it is this innate spirit that has led me to embrace the digital nomad lifestyle.

Modern life, with its constraints and discriminatory systems surrounding my culture, left me feeling confined and restricted. The options presented within the rat race of the United Kingdom felt limiting and unsatisfying. However, my path took an unexpected turn when my work in human rights and social housing roles led me to partnerships and conferences throughout Europe. These experiences ignited a spark within me, unveiling the possibilities of living and working in different places.

It was during my time in Albania that I truly discovered the power of online work. Faced with the need to support myself and my daughters, I delved into the world of digital nomadism, utilizing my skills to teach English online, practice tarot and astrology, and explore various other income streams. With each passing year, my life in Tunisia beckoned me closer, and I made the life-altering decision to embrace the digital nomad lifestyle in its entirety.

From the enchanting beaches of Sousse in Tunisia, I found myself living in a villa, where the rhythmic waves served as the soundtrack to my work. It was a paradise where I funded my children's education, their lives, and my own, all while revelling in the freedom to pursue my passions on my own terms. The beauty of it all was that it never felt like work. Writing, which I have always adored, seamlessly merged with my nomadic existence, allowing me to embrace my love for storytelling and expression.

Now, as I reflect on my journey, I am inspired to share my experiences, insights, and the lessons learned along the way. It is my fervent belief that if I, a Gypsy with an inherent desire for exploration and a profound connection to nature, can embark on this extraordinary path and find fulfilment, then anyone with a yearning to traverse the globe, savour its beauty, and enjoy the fruits of their labour under their own terms can do the same.

Within the pages of this book, you will find guidance, practical advice, and a gentle nudge to step outside the confines of societal expectations. I invite you to embrace the unknown, dissolve the limitations, and discover the boundless opportunities that await you as a digital nomad. May these words serve as a beacon of inspiration, guiding you towards a life of adventure, self-discovery, and the pursuit of your passions.

With love and wanderlust,

Jane-Ann Koci

CHAPTER 1: INTRODUCTION TO DIGITAL NOMADISM

Hello there, adventurous spirit! Welcome to the exciting world of digital nomadism, a lifestyle that combines work, travel, and the freedom to live pretty much anywhere you want. But before you start packing your bags for Bali or booking that one-way ticket to Barcelona, let's delve into what being a digital nomad truly means.

So, what's a digital nomad, you ask? Well, it's not a new type of migratory bird, nor is it a coding wizard traveling on a camel's back through the Sahara (though that would be quite a sight!). A digital nomad is simply someone who works remotely, utilizing technology to perform their job, all while embracing a location-independent lifestyle that allows them to travel and live wherever they choose.

Sounds like the dream, right? Well, while it's true that the digital nomad lifestyle can be incredibly rewarding, it's not all sunshine, coconuts, and Instagram-worthy sunsets. There are Wi-Fi woes, time zone tangles, and the ever-present search for the perfect cup of coffee. But hey, who doesn't love a good adventure?

Let's bust some myths. No, you don't have to be a 20-something Instagram influencer or a tech-savvy app developer to join the digital nomad club. People of all ages, backgrounds, and professions are embracing this lifestyle - teachers, writers, marketers, accountants, and yes, even grandmas with a knack for graphic design!

On the flip side, being a digital nomad isn't a perpetual vacation. It's not about lounging on the beach with your laptop (sand and electronics don't mix well, trust me). It's about balancing work with exploration, mastering the art of time management, and occasionally struggling to explain to customs officials that yes, you work on that small screen, and no, you're not involved in any shady business.

There's also a fantastic community aspect to this lifestyle. You might find yourself having deep conversations with fellow nomads over shared co-working spaces or exchanging tips and experiences at digital nomad meetups. One day, you could be brainstorming business ideas with a fellow nomad in Lisbon, and the next, you might be practicing yoga with a group in Chiang Mai.

The digital nomad lifestyle is like a choose-your-own-adventure book, but instead of turning pages, you're booking flights, exploring cultures, and creating a life that resonates with your own rhythm and pace. So, if you're ready to swap your office cubicle for a beach cabana in Mexico or a bustling café in the heart of Tokyo, you're in the right place.

In the coming chapters, we'll explore how you can transition to this thrilling way of life, including practical tips, essential tools, and a whole lot of encouragement. So buckle up, future nomads, because we're about to embark on an exciting journey into the wide world of digital nomadism!

Next stop: Chapter 2, where we'll delve into the crucial skills every digital nomad needs to master. Spoiler alert: being able to order coffee in five different languages is one of them. Just kidding... or am I? Stick around to find out!

CHAPTER 2: ESSENTIAL SKILLS FOR DIGITAL NOMADS

Welcome back, wanderlust warrior! Now that we've dipped our toes into the alluring pool of digital nomadism, it's time to equip ourselves with the essential skills needed to thrive in this lifestyle. And no, I'm not talking about learning how to make a coconut shell into a Wi-Fi booster (though if you figure it out, do share!).

Let's dive into the top skills that will make your digital nomad journey smoother, more productive, and let's be real, a whole lot more fun.

1. Time Management: The digital nomad lifestyle can be a dazzling whirlwind of work, travel, and exploring new cultures. It's easy to lose track of time when you're strolling through the vibrant markets of Marrakech or surfing the waves in Costa Rica. But remember, deadlines wait for no nomad! Mastering the art of managing your time is crucial. You might be in paradise, but that report still needs to be submitted by Monday morning.

2. Self-discipline: Freedom and flexibility are the hallmarks of digital nomadism, but with great freedom comes great responsibility. Without the structure of a traditional office environment, it's up to you to create a productive work routine.

This means not hitting snooze on your alarm just because you had a late-night salsa dancing session (no matter how tempting it might be!).

3. Tech-savviness: As a digital nomad, technology is your lifeline. From ensuring a stable internet connection for that important Zoom call to troubleshooting laptop issues, being comfortable with technology is a must. You don't need to be the next Steve Jobs, but knowing your way around your gadgets is essential.

4. Communication: You might be solo travelling, but communication is still key. You'll need to maintain open lines with your clients, colleagues, or team, regardless of the time zones. Also, having some basic language skills of the country you're in will go a long way. Remember when I joked about ordering coffee in five languages? Well, it's not entirely a joke!

5. Adaptability: As a digital nomad, change is the only constant. Flights get delayed, Wi-Fi goes down, and yes, sometimes you do end up in a city where no one seems to understand the concept of decaf coffee. Being adaptable and flexible will help you navigate these challenges with grace (and minimal caffeine withdrawal symptoms!).

6. Networking: Building relationships with other digital nomads can lead to new opportunities, collaborations, and let's not forget, some great travel buddies. Attend local meetups, join online communities, and don't be shy to strike up a conversation with that fellow nomad at your co-working space.

7. Financial Management: Budgeting and financial planning are crucial when you're living a location-independent lifestyle. Understanding the cost of living in your chosen destinations, tracking your expenses, and planning for the unexpected are all part of being a financially savvy digital nomad.

So there you have it, the essential skill set of a successful digital nomad. No one expects you to be a master of all these skills right off the bat, but developing them will definitely put you in good stead for your digital nomad journey.

Next up, we'll be venturing into Chapter 3, where we'll discuss the various job opportunities that can fund your digital nomad lifestyle. Spoiler alert: you won't need to sell coconuts on the beach (unless that's your passion, of course!).

CHAPTER 3: FINDING REMOTE WORK

Hello again, intrepid adventurer! We've mastered the essential skills, now it's time to find a job that will fund your digital nomad dreams. But where do you start? Don't worry, I've got you covered.

Let's delve into the wide world of remote work and discover the opportunities awaiting you. And no, none of them involve selling seashells by the seashore (although that does have a certain poetic charm).

1. Freelancing: This is the bread and butter of many digital nomads. Are you a wizard with words? A graphic design guru? Awe software savant? Then freelancing could be your ticket to nomad nirvana. Websites like Upwork, Fiverr, and Freelancer are great places to start looking for gigs. Remember to showcase your portfolio and don't undersell your skills.

2. Remote Employee: Yes, you can have a traditional job while being a digital nomad! More and more companies are embracing remote work, especially post-COVID. Websites like Remote.co, We Work Remotely, and FlexJobs list job postings from companies looking for remote employees.

3. Teaching or Tutoring: If you have a knack for teaching, why not become an online tutor? You could teach English, mathematics, coding, music, or any other subject you're knowledgeable in. Websites like VIPKid and Chegg Tutors are great platforms for finding students.

4. Blogging or Vlogging: Got a captivating story to tell or a unique perspective to share? Start a blog or a YouTube channel. It's not a quick money-making scheme, but with consistency and quality content, it can turn into a lucrative career. Remember, every successful blogger started with a single post or video.

5. eCommerce: Got a product to sell? It could be handmade jewellery, digital prints, or even a recipe book of dishes you've discovered on your travels. Set up an online store on platforms like Etsy or Shopify.

6. Affiliate Marketing: This involves promoting other people's products and earning a commission on any sales made through your referral link. If you have a sizable social media following or a blog with substantial traffic, this could be a profitable option.

7. Consultancy: If you have years of experience in a certain field, why not use that knowledge to guide others? As a consultant, you could offer advice and solutions to clients in your area of expertise.

8. Virtual Assistance: Good at organization and administrative tasks? Companies and entrepreneurs often hire virtual assistants to handle tasks such as email management, scheduling, customer service, and more.

Remember, the key to finding the perfect remote job is to match your skills and interests with the needs of potential employers or clients. And remember, patience is key. It might take some time to land the perfect gig, but don't get disheartened. Your dream job is out there, waiting for you.

Next, in Chapter 4, we'll delve into how to stay productive while being a digital nomad. Spoiler alert: it involves more than just strong coffee (though that definitely helps!).

CHAPTER 4: MASTERING PRODUCTIVITY IN PARADISE

Well hello, future digital nomad! So, you've got the skills and you've found your remote work, but how do you stay productive when the beach is calling your name? Or when the local market has the freshest of fruits that you just must try? Fear not, productivity is not as elusive as it may seem, even in paradise. Let's dive in.

1. Establish a Routine: Yes, the beauty of being a digital nomad is the freedom from a 9-5 routine, but having some structure can help boost productivity. This doesn't mean you need to work 8 hours straight. Find a routine that suits your lifestyle and stick to it. Remember, you're not just working remotely, you're living remotely.

2. Time Management: Ever heard of the Pomodoro Technique? It involves working for a set amount of time (usually 25 minutes), then taking a short break, and repeating. This can help prevent burnout and keep you focused. Also, consider using tools like Google Calendar or Trello to keep track of your tasks and deadlines.

3. Find Your Ideal Workspace: While working from a hammock under a palm tree sounds idyllic, it may not be the most practical. Seek out places where you can work comfortably and with minimal distractions, whether that's a café, a co-working space, or your accommodation.

4. Stay Connected: Reliable internet is the lifeline of a digital nomad. Always have a backup plan in case your internet connection fails. This could involve knowing the locations of local cafes or co-working spaces, or investing in a good quality mobile hotspot.

5. Take Care of Your Health: It's easy to get so wrapped up in work and exploration that you neglect your health. But remember, a healthy body fuels a productive mind. Ensure you're eating well, getting enough sleep, and fitting in some exercise (like that beach yoga class you've been eyeing).

6. Set Boundaries: Just because you can work anytime, doesn't mean you should. Set boundaries for your work time and personal time. Know when to log off and go explore that hidden waterfall or local festival.

7. Stay Motivated: It can be hard to stay motivated when you're far from your team or clients. Find what keeps you driven and incorporate it into your routine. Maybe it's a morning run, a mid-day break to read, or a rewarding end-of-the-week local treat.

8. Networking: Connect with other digital nomads. Not only is this a great way to make friends, but it also helps in staying motivated and sharing tips and advice. Check out local meetups or online communities like Nomad List.

Staying productive as a digital nomad is a delicate balance of work, play, and self-care. It might take a bit of trial and error to find your groove, but once you do, you'll be unstoppable.

In the next chapter, we'll discuss how to navigate the tricky world of finances as a digital nomad. Spoiler alert: it involves more than just stashing your cash under your mattress (though if you find a mattress that comes with a cash stash, let me know!).

CHAPTER 5: FINANCIAL PLANNING FOR DIGITAL NOMADS

Ah, finance - everyone's favourite topic! As a digital nomad, managing your finances can be slightly more complex than for those living a stationary lifestyle. However, with a bit of planning and the right tools, you can keep your money in order while gallivanting around the globe.

1. Budgeting: Start with a realistic and flexible budget. It should account for all your anticipated costs, such as accommodation, food, insurance, travel expenses, and even some budget for unexpected costs or emergencies. Remember, cost of living can vary greatly from one location to the next, so be ready to adjust your budget as you move.

2. Track Your Spending: Keep a record of all your expenses. It's easy to lose track of your spending when you're hopping from one place to another, but understanding where your money is going is crucial for maintaining financial health. There are plenty of mobile apps available that can help you track your spending.

3. Diversify Your Income: Having multiple income streams is a great way to ensure financial stability. This could mean taking on multiple clients or projects, or having passive income streams like affiliate marketing or investment returns.

4. Taxes: Ah, the joy of taxes. As a digital nomad, your tax situation can be a bit more complex. The rules vary depending on your nationality, your country of residence, and where you earn your income. It may be worthwhile to consult with a tax professional who is familiar with the nuances of taxes for digital nomads.

5. Banking and Money Transfers: When it comes to banking, things can get a bit tricky for digital nomads. Look for banks that offer services online and have low international transaction fees. Consider using money transfer services like TransferWise or Revolut, which offer competitive exchange rates and low fees.

6. Health and Travel Insurance: Don't forget about insurance! Ensure you have a comprehensive health insurance plan that covers you internationally. Also consider getting travel insurance to cover potential travel-related mishaps like lost luggage or trip cancellations.

7. Save for Retirement: Yes, even digital nomads need to think about retirement. Look into setting up a self-employed retirement plan. Remember, the earlier you start saving, the better.

8. Emergency Fund: Having money set aside for emergencies is crucial, especially when you're living a nomadic lifestyle. Aim to save enough to cover at least 3-6 months' worth of expenses.

Remember, financial planning is not a one-time task, but an ongoing process. Regularly review and adjust your plan as needed. After all, financial stability is one of the keys to maintaining your digital nomad lifestyle in the long run.

Next up, we'll tackle another crucial topic: choosing your destination. Spoiler alert: it involves more than just sending postcards (but please, do send postcards, they're lovely!).

CHAPTER 6: CHOOSING YOUR DESTINATION

Congratulations, fellow nomad! You've honed your skills, found remote work, set your finances straight, and are now ready to embark on your digital nomad journey. But wait, where should you go first? That's what this chapter is all about: choosing your perfect destination.

1. Determine Your Priorities: Everyone has different priorities when choosing a destination. Some people might prioritize a low cost of living, while others might want a destination with a vibrant digital nomad community. Maybe you're looking for a city with a thriving art scene, or perhaps you're a foodie who wants to explore a country with a rich culinary history. Take some time to figure out what matters most to you.

2. Cost of Living: As we mentioned in the financial planning chapter, the cost of living can vary greatly from one location to the next. Websites like Nomad List and Cost of Living Index can give you a rough idea of how much it will cost to live in different cities around the world.

3. Internet Connectivity: You're a digital nomad, after all. Reliable internet is a must. Research the internet connectivity of your potential destinations. Remember, a beach in Bali might look like paradise, but if you can't get a steady Wi-Fi signal, it might be more of a headache than a haven.

4. Safety: Safety should always be a priority. Use resources like the Global Peace Index and travel advisories from your home country's foreign affairs department to gauge the safety of potential destinations.

5. Local Culture and Language: Living in a different country means adapting to a new culture and possibly a new language. Some research on the local culture, customs, and etiquette can help you integrate and have a richer experience.

6. Climate: Some people thrive in tropical climates, while others prefer a cooler environment. Consider the climate of your potential destinations and think about where you'd be most comfortable.

7. Visa Regulations: Last but definitely not least, always check the visa regulations of the countries you're considering. Some countries offer digital nomad visas that allow you to live and work there legally.

Choosing your destination is a big decision, but remember, one of the best parts of being a digital nomad is that nothing is permanent. If you arrive somewhere and it's not what you expected, you can always pack up and move on. That's the beauty of this lifestyle – the world is your oyster.

In the next chapter, we'll discuss housing and accommodation, how to prepare for the move and what to pack. Spoiler alert: you probably need less than you think!

CHAPTER 7: HOUSING AND ACCOMMODATION

Alright, future globetrotter! You've got your skills, your remote job, your finances in order, and you've chosen your destination. Now comes the next big question: where are you going to live? Let's discuss some of the options available and how to find a place that suits your needs.

1. Short-Term Rentals: Websites like Airbnb, Booking.com, and Agoda are popular options for digital nomads. They offer a wide range of accommodation options, from shared rooms to entire apartments or houses. They also provide the flexibility to book for a few days, weeks, or even months at a time.

2. Long-Term Rentals: If you're planning to stay in a location for an extended period, consider looking for a long-term rental. Websites like Apartments.com, Rightmove (UK), or Craigslist can be a good place to start. In some countries, it might be best to hire a local real estate agent to help you navigate the process.

3. Co-Living Spaces: These are becoming increasingly popular among digital nomads. Co-living spaces are shared housing arrangements where residents rent a private room but share common areas like the kitchen, living room, and sometimes even workspaces. These can be great for meeting other digital nomads and for those who don't want to deal with setting up utilities or furnishing an apartment.

4. Hostels: For those on a tight budget or looking for a more social environment, hostels can be a good option. Many hostels offer private rooms in addition to dorm-style accommodations, and some even have co-working spaces.

5. Hotels: Some digital nomads prefer to stay in hotels, especially if they're only going to be in a location for a short time. Many hotels offer discounted rates for extended stays.

6. House Sitting: Websites like TrustedHousesitters connect homeowners who are going to be away with individuals willing to look after their home and sometimes their pets. In exchange for taking care of the house, the house sitter gets to stay for free.

7. Checking the Basics: No matter where you choose to stay, make sure to check the basics: reliable Wi-Fi, a comfortable workspace, safety, and proximity to amenities like grocery stores, restaurants, and public transportation.

8. Reviews are Your Friends: Always check reviews before booking a place. Reviews can provide valuable insights about the reliability of the internet, the comfort of the living space, the neighbourhood, and the responsiveness of the host.

In the end, the best housing option for you will depend on your budget, your lifestyle, and your personal preferences. Remember, part of the adventure is finding a place you can call home, even if it's only for a short while.

In the next chapter, we'll dive into digital nomadism with a family, is it possible to travel and work with kids? Check it out to find out.

CHAPTER 8: DIGITAL NOMADISM WITH A FAMILY

Alright, digital nomad parents, this one's for you. You might be wondering, "Can I really do this with kids in tow?" The answer is a resounding yes! Let's talk about how to navigate the world of digital nomadism with your little (or not so little) ones.

1. Education: One of the first things you're probably thinking about is schooling. You have several options here:

  * **Home-schooling:** Many nomad families choose to home-school their children. This provides a lot of flexibility and can be an enriching experience as your children can learn from the different cultures and environments they encounter. There are numerous online resources and curriculums to help you with this.

  * **International Schools:** If you plan to stay in one location for an extended period, you might consider enrolling your children in an international school. These schools often offer a curriculum recognized worldwide.

  * **Worldschooling:** This is a combination of travel and education where the world becomes your child's classroom. It's about making the most of the educational opportunities that

naturally occur while travelling.

2. Socialization: It's important for kids to interact with their peers. Look for local activities, clubs, or sports teams in the area. Websites like Meetup can be a useful resource to find local groups.

3. Health Care: Always ensure you have adequate health insurance that will cover your family in whatever country you're in. Regular check-ups can be scheduled during times you're back in your home country or in locations with high-quality medical care.

4. Making it Fun: Remember, this is an adventure! Involve your kids in the planning process, let them help choose destinations, and find attractions or activities in each location that they'll enjoy.

5. Staying Connected: Just because you're on the move doesn't mean you can't stay connected with your family and friends. Regular video calls can help your children maintain relationships and feel connected to their home base.

6. Accommodation: When choosing accommodation, look for family-friendly options. Many short-term rental sites allow you to filter for family-friendly accommodations, which can include anything from having cribs available to being located near a playground.

7. Balance: As a digital nomad parent, you'll need to balance work, education, and exploration. It can help to create a flexible routine that gives structure to your days but also allows for spontaneity.

CHAPTER 9:
CULTIVATING
CONNECTIONS
ON THE ROAD TO
DIGITAL NOMADISM

Greetings, fellow adventurers! As digital nomads, we embark on a thrilling journey that allows us to cross paths with individuals from all walks of life. However, the constant movement can present challenges when it comes to building a sense of community. Fear not, for we are here to guide you on how to forge meaningful connections and create a harmonious work-life balance, no matter where your wanderlust takes you.

1. Embracing Co-living and Co-working Spaces:

Co-living Spaces: These vibrant residential buildings offer a home away from home for digital nomads. By providing private rooms alongside shared communal areas, they foster an instant community of like-minded individuals who understand the nomadic lifestyle.

Co-working Spaces: Just like co-living spaces, co-working spaces are havens for digital nomads seeking a productive work environment. These workspaces not only provide a dedicated workspace but also offer networking opportunities and organize social events, eliminating the need to feel guilty about occupying a café table for hours on end.

2. Leveraging Social Media and Networking Apps:

Facebook Groups: The digital realm boasts an array of Facebook groups dedicated to the thriving digital nomad community. Engaging with these groups allows you to ask questions, share experiences, and even organize meet-ups with fellow nomads in your current location or future destinations.

Apps: Discover the power of platforms like Meetup, Couchsurfing, and Nomad List, designed to connect you with other travellers and locals alike. These apps enable you to join local events, explore cultural activities, and find the perfect city to embrace your digital nomad lifestyle.

3. Immersing in Local Events and Activities:

Community Events: Immerse yourself in the vibrancy of local festivals, yoga classes, or cultural gatherings. Participating in these activities not only deepens your connection with the local culture but also provides opportunities to meet fascinating individuals who share your passion for exploration.

Language Exchanges: Unlock the joy of language exchanges, where individuals gather to practice different languages. These delightful gatherings offer a fun and free way to make friends while simultaneously expanding your linguistic skills and connecting with locals on a deeper level.

4. Embracing Volunteering Opportunities:

Local Projects: Engaging in volunteer work within the local community not only allows you to contribute meaningfully but also offers a rewarding avenue to connect with both locals and fellow travellers. By dedicating your time and skills to local projects, you cultivate bonds and create a positive impact wherever you go.

5. Nurturing Connections Across Distances:

Staying Connected: The beauty of modern technology lies in its ability to bridge distances. Through social media platforms and video calls, maintaining relationships with your newfound global network has never been easier. Regular catch-ups and virtual gatherings keep connections alive, no matter how many miles separate you. Who knows, your stories and experiences might inspire someone else to embark on their own remarkable digital nomad journey!

With these invaluable strategies, building a community while traversing the nomadic path may seem less daunting. By investing effort and utilizing the right resources, you will find yourself surrounded by a diverse and supportive network of friends and colleagues. In the following chapter, we will delve into the practical aspects of staying connected abroad. Stay tuned, fellow adventurers!

CHAPTER 10: STAYING CONNECTED: INTERNET AND COMMUNICATION

Hello, dear future digital nomads! Let's chat about the lifeline of your nomadic existence: the Internet. Without it, the whole digital nomad thing kind of falls apart. And it's not just about work – it's also about staying connected to your loved ones, accessing essential services, and more. Let's dive in!

1. Getting Online:

* **Local SIM Cards:** Purchasing a local SIM card when you land in a new country is often the cheapest way to get data on your phone. Just make sure your phone is unlocked first!

* **Portable Wi-Fi Devices:** Devices like Skyroam or GlocalMe provide you with internet access in many countries. You pay for the data you use, and it can be shared among several devices.

* **Internet Cafes and Co-working Spaces:** These are popular options, especially in cities. They offer reliable internet and a good working environment. Some even offer meeting rooms and other resources.

2. Staying in Touch:

* **Social Media:** Platforms like Instagram, Facebook, and Twitter are great ways to share your adventures and stay connected with your loved ones.

* **Video Calls:** Services like Skype, Zoom, and FaceTime are fantastic for video calling. Regular video chats can help you stay close to your family and friends, even when you're thousands of miles away.

* **Blogging:** Consider starting a blog. It's a great way to document your journey and keep folks back home in the loop. Plus, it could even turn into a source of income!

3. Essential Services:

* **Banking:** Online banking is your friend. Make sure you have a bank that offers online services, such as money transfers and bill payments. Also, consider getting a credit card that doesn't charge foreign transaction fees.

* **Health Services:** Telemedicine is becoming more and more popular. It allows you to consult with healthcare professionals over the phone or through video calls. Make sure you have a good health insurance policy that covers international care.

* **Mail:** Use a virtual mailbox service. These services provide you with a physical address where you can receive mail. They'll then scan it and send it to you digitally.

4. Safety:

* **VPN:** A Virtual Private Network (VPN) can provide an extra layer of security when you're accessing the internet, especially on public networks. It also allows you to access services that might be region-locked.

* **Password Managers:** These tools store all your passwords securely, so you only need to remember one. They can also generate strong, unique passwords for each of your accounts.

There you have it, folks! Staying connected while living the digital nomad lifestyle is not just possible; it's easier than you might think. Next up, we'll discuss ways to maintain health and wellness while living in different countries. Stay tuned!

CHAPTER 11: MAINTAINING HEALTH AND WELLNESS

Well hello, digital nomad! You've been gallivanting around the globe, working, exploring, making new friends, and immersing yourself in diverse cultures. But have you stopped to consider your health and wellness amidst all this excitement? Maintaining your well-being is paramount, and this chapter will guide you on how to stay healthy and happy on your nomadic journey.

1. Nutrition:

* **Cooking for Yourself:** Opting to prepare your own meals not only saves money but also allows you to control what goes into your body. Whenever possible, try to cook with local, fresh ingredients.

* **Eating Out Smartly:** When you do eat out, choose places where food is fresh and hygienic. Look for spots where locals eat - they usually know the best places!

2. Exercise:

* **Workout Routines:** Even if you don't have access to a gym, there are plenty of workout routines available online that require

no equipment.

* **Outdoor Activities:** Make the most of your surroundings. Go for a hike, swim in the sea, cycle through the city. It's a great way to keep fit while exploring.

3. Mental Health:

* **Keeping a Routine:** Establishing a routine can provide a sense of normalcy and control, which is important for mental well-being.

* **Mindfulness and Meditation:** Practicing mindfulness or meditation can help manage stress and anxiety. There are plenty of mobile apps available to guide you.

4. Sleep:

* **Quality Sleep:** Prioritize getting enough quality sleep. This may mean investing in a good eye mask and earplugs or choosing accommodations in quieter areas.

5. Healthcare:

* **Travel Insurance:** Make sure your travel insurance covers healthcare in the countries you're visiting.

* **Routine Checkups:** If you're staying in one place for a while, consider getting a routine medical and dental check-up. It's better to catch potential issues early.

6. Stay Hydrated:

* **Drinking Water:** Always stay hydrated, but make sure the water you're drinking is safe. If in doubt, opt for bottled water.

7. Moderation:

* **Balance:** It's okay to let loose and enjoy yourself, but remember to balance work, play, rest, and self-care.

There you have it, my health-conscious wanderers. Your health and wellness are just as important as your work and adventures. The healthier you are, the more you can enjoy your digital nomad lifestyle. Stay fit, stay well, and continue to explore this magnificent world of ours! Up next, we'll navigate the tricky waters or challenges of the digital nomad life, so hang tight!

CHAPTER 12: OVERCOMING CHALLENGES OF THE DIGITAL NOMAD LIFE

Alright, my nomadic warriors! You're living the dream, working from beautiful locations and experiencing cultures beyond your wildest imaginations. But it's not all sunshine and coconuts, is it? The digital nomad life comes with its own set of challenges. Let's arm ourselves with the knowledge to overcome these bumps in the road.

1. Loneliness:

* **Build Connections:** Regularly attend meetups, co-working spaces, and local events. Engaging with others can lead to meaningful friendships and a strong support network.

* **Stay Connected:** Regular video calls with friends and family back home can do wonders for your morale.

2. Unreliable Internet:

* **Backup Plans:** Always have a backup option for the internet.

This could be a local SIM card, portable Wi-Fi device, or a list of nearby cafes with good Wi-Fi.

* **Offline Work:** Have tasks that can be done offline, so even without internet, you can stay productive.

3. Health Issues:

* **Preparation:** Have a basic first aid kit, know the location of the nearest hospital, and keep emergency contact numbers handy.

* **Insurance:** Ensure your health insurance covers you internationally.

4. Language Barriers:

* **Learning Basics:** Learn a few basic phrases in the local language. This not only helps in daily life but also shows respect for the local culture.

* **Translation Apps:** Utilize translation apps to help communicate more effectively.

5. Time Zone Differences:

* **Scheduling:** Use tools that help you manage time zone differences for meetings and deadlines.

* **Balance:** Ensure you're balancing work commitments with the need for rest. Don't let different time zones disrupt your sleep patterns.

6. Financial Management:

* **Budgeting:** Keep track of your expenses and have a budget. Costs can quickly add up when you're moving between countries.

* **Emergency Funds:** Always have an emergency fund for unexpected costs.

7. Visa Issues:

* **Research:** Always research visa requirements before entering a country. Staying beyond your visa limit can lead to serious consequences.

* **Professional Help:** Consider using a visa service if the process is too complex or time-consuming.

8. Burnout:

* **Self-care:** Make sure you're taking time for yourself and not just working or exploring.

* **Rest Days:** Schedule regular rest days where you don't work or travel, just relax.

Life on the road can be tough, but remember, what doesn't kill you makes you stronger... or at least gives you a good story to tell at the next digital nomad meetup! By acknowledging these challenges and preparing for them, you're well on your way to mastering the digital nomad life. Ready for the next step? Our next chapter will delve into returning home and transitioning out of the nomadic lifestyle. Until then, happy nomading!

CHAPTER 13: MY DIGITAL NOMAD SUCCESS STORY

Greetings, fellow adventurers! In this chapter, I am thrilled to share my personal success story as a digital nomad, a journey that has transformed my life in remarkable ways. Join me as I take you through the captivating destinations and experiences that have shaped my nomadic path.

My name is Jane-Ann Koci, and my digital nomad journey began in the stunning landscapes of Albania. Albania captured my heart with its rich history, warm hospitality, and untamed beauty. It was here that I first discovered the liberating potential of working remotely while immersing myself in a new culture and embracing the charms of a slower-paced lifestyle.

As I continued my nomadic adventure, I found myself drawn to the vibrant shores of Tunisia. This North African gem became my temporary home, where I revelled in the harmonious blend of ancient traditions and modern influences. Living amidst the breath-taking Mediterranean landscapes, I found solace in the tranquil beauty of olive trees, the fragrance of citrus groves, and the gentle breeze that whispered tales of distant lands.

While my nomadic journey has taken me to various corners of

the globe, I am currently rooted in the United Kingdom. Here, my daughter is undertaking her exams, seizing the opportunity to excel academically before we embark on our next grand adventure in Spain. The UK is our home, although we've enjoyed some time back with family and friends, camping trips and family holidays it is providing the perfect backdrop for our temporary stay.

In the coming months, we eagerly anticipate our transition to Spain, a land of passionate flamenco, awe-inspiring architecture, and sun-kissed Mediterranean beaches. It is a destination that beckons with its vibrant culture, friendly locals, and a tantalizing blend of ancient history and modern delights. Our hearts are brimming with excitement as we prepare to immerse ourselves in the Spanish way of life, embracing new experiences and connecting with fellow nomads on this journey of discovery.

While my digital nomad lifestyle has been a source of immense joy and fulfilment, it hasn't been without its share of challenges. Balancing work responsibilities, providing my daughter with a well-rounded education, and nurturing our wanderlust can be demanding at times. However, through careful planning, effective time management, and a commitment to maintaining a healthy work-life balance, I have managed to navigate these obstacles and continue thriving in the nomadic lifestyle.

My success story as a digital nomad extends beyond professional achievements. It encompasses the precious moments of connection, personal growth, and cultural immersion that have enriched my life and broadened my horizons. Whether it's savouring the flavours of Albanian cuisine, exploring the historical treasures of Tunisia, or embracing the vibrant energy of the UK, each destination has woven its unique tapestry into the fabric of my journey.

As you embark on your own digital nomad adventure, I hope my story serves as inspiration and encouragement. Embrace the freedom to explore new horizons, seize the opportunities that lie ahead, and create a life that resonates with your deepest desires. The world is a vast tapestry of wonders, waiting to be discovered. Embrace the unknown, embrace the nomadic spirit, and let your journey unfold with passion and purpose.

Safe travels, fellow adventurers, and may your digital nomad journey be filled with boundless opportunities and unforgettable experiences.

Yes, traveling full-time with a family has its challenges, but the rewards are immeasurable. The experiences your children will have and the education they'll receive are unlike anything they would get in a traditional lifestyle. So go forth and show your children the world!

In the next chapter, we'll talk about how to maintain a healthy work-life balance while being a digital nomad. Stay tuned!

CHAPTER 14: THE FUTURE OF DIGITAL NOMADISM

As we journey further into the 21st century, it's clear that the landscape of work is rapidly changing. The advent of the digital nomad lifestyle has been a prominent part of this shift. As we look towards the future, it's exciting to consider the potential evolution and impact of digital nomadism.

Firstly, technology will undoubtedly continue to be a significant driving force in the future of digital nomadism. The proliferation of high-speed internet, the rise of cloud computing, and the development of even more efficient digital tools will further enable remote work. This will not only enhance the productivity of digital nomads but also allow for greater flexibility and mobility.

Moreover, the COVID-19 pandemic has already accelerated the trend towards remote work, with many companies realizing the benefits of having a remote workforce. This may lead to an increase in the number of digital nomads, as more people and businesses adopt flexible work arrangements.

Furthermore, it is expected that governments and cities worldwide will increasingly recognize the economic benefits of attracting digital nomads. We may see the development of more "digital nomad visas" and initiatives designed to make countries more appealing to remote workers. For instance, Estonia has already introduced a digital nomad visa, and countries like Barbados and Georgia have followed suit.

Education is also likely to adapt to accommodate this lifestyle, with an increase in online learning options for children of digital nomads. International schools and universities may offer more flexible programs, and home-schooling resources could become more prevalent.

However, as digital nomadism continues to grow, so will its challenges. Issues such as maintaining work-life balance, dealing with isolation, and managing health care across different countries will need to be addressed. As a result, we might see the rise of support services and communities tailored to the needs of digital nomads.

Finally, as the number of digital nomads grows, so too will their impact on the environment. This raises questions about how digital nomadism can become more sustainable, from carbon-neutral travel options to more sustainable accommodation choices.

In conclusion, the future of digital nomadism is exciting and full of potential. It promises more freedom, flexibility, and opportunities for exploration than ever before. However, it also calls for thoughtful solutions to its unique challenges. As we step into this future, it will be fascinating to see how digital nomadism continues to shape our world.

CHAPTER 15: CONCLUSION - EMBRACING THE DIGITAL NOMAD LIFESTYLE

As we conclude this guide, it's important to reflect on the profound potential that the digital nomad lifestyle holds. Embracing this lifestyle means opening yourself to new experiences, cultures, and ways of thinking that can enrich your life beyond measure.

The digital nomad lifestyle is about more than just work or travel. It's about embracing a mindset of flexibility, adaptability, and continuous learning. It's about recognizing that our traditional notions of work and life may be ready for an update, and that technology has given us the tools to make this possible.

However, embracing the digital nomad lifestyle is not without its challenges. The journey will require careful planning, perseverance, and resilience. It means stepping out of comfort zones, navigating different cultures, and sometimes dealing with uncertainty. Yet, these challenges can also become the most rewarding aspects of the journey, fostering personal growth and resilience.

Moreover, embracing this lifestyle means being part of a global community of like-minded individuals. Digital nomads are a diverse group, coming from different backgrounds and cultures, yet they share a common desire for freedom, flexibility, and adventure. This community can provide support, friendship, and inspiration as you navigate your own digital nomad journey.

As we move into the future, the digital nomad lifestyle will likely become even more accessible and prevalent. More businesses are recognizing the value of remote work, and more countries are opening their doors to digital nomads. Meanwhile, technological advancements will continue to make remote work more efficient and enjoyable.

In conclusion, embracing the digital nomad lifestyle is about embracing the future of work—a future that values freedom, flexibility, and the balance between work and life. It's about recognizing that we have the power to shape our work life to suit our needs and desires, rather than the other way around. Whether you're dreaming of working from a beach in Bali, a cafe in Paris, or a mountain cabin in Colorado, the digital nomad lifestyle is a step towards turning those dreams into reality. It is a journey, and like all journeys, it begins with a single step. Here's to taking that step and embracing the digital nomad lifestyle!

RESOURCES FOR DIGITAL NOMADS

Bloggers:

1. Nomadic Matt: A renowned digital nomad blogger who has been traveling the world for over a decade. Nomadic Matt shares his experiences and provides valuable tips on his blog, guiding aspiring digital nomads on their own journeys.

2. Location Rebel: This popular blog offers a wealth of resources and advice for individuals who aspire to work remotely while exploring the world. Location Rebel covers topics ranging from freelancing to building online businesses, providing practical insights for aspiring digital nomads.

3. Escape from Cubicle Nation: Authored by a former corporate lawyer who left her job to embark on a nomadic lifestyle, Escape from Cubicle Nation offers inspiring stories and actionable tips on breaking free from the traditional work paradigm. This blog encourages individuals to escape the rat race and pursue a more fulfilling life.

Websites:

1. NomadList: A comprehensive website that ranks cities worldwide based on factors important to digital nomads, such as cost of living, internet speed, safety, and quality of life. NomadList assists in choosing the ideal destination for your next nomadic

adventure.

2. Remote Year: If you seek a structured approach to your nomadic journey, Remote Year offers a program that allows participants to travel to 12 different countries over the course of one year while working remotely. It provides a supportive community and takes care of logistics, allowing you to focus on work and exploration.

3. Digital Nomad Academy: For those looking for in-depth guidance on becoming a digital nomad, the Digital Nomad Academy offers online courses that cover various aspects of the lifestyle. From building remote income streams to managing finances while traveling, the academy provides valuable knowledge to set you up for success.

Communities:

1. Digital Nomads Facebook Group: Engage with a vibrant community of digital nomads on this Facebook group. Connect with like-minded individuals, ask questions, share experiences, and benefit from the collective wisdom of the community.

2. Digital Nomads Reddit Forum: Join the Reddit forum dedicated to digital nomads, where you can participate in discussions, seek advice, and share your own insights. This forum provides a platform for connecting with a diverse community of digital nomads from around the world.

3. Digital Nomads Meetup Group: Utilize the Meetup platform to find local digital nomad communities in your area. Attend events, meet fellow nomads, and foster connections with individuals who share your passion for location independence and remote work.

These resources will equip you with valuable insights, support, and connections as you embark on your digital nomad journey. Remember to explore these platforms, engage with the community, and make the most of the vast knowledge and experiences shared by fellow nomads. Safe travels and may your adventures be filled with joy, growth, and unforgettable memories!

Here are some recommended tools and apps for digital nomads to enhance productivity, communication, organization, and overall convenience while working and traveling:

1. Communication and Collaboration:

- Slack: A popular messaging and collaboration platform that allows for easy communication with remote teams and fellow nomads.

- Zoom: A reliable video conferencing tool for virtual meetings, client calls, and team collaboration.

- Trello: A project management tool that helps organize tasks, track progress, and collaborate with others.

- Google Drive: A cloud storage platform for storing and sharing files, documents, and presentations.

2. Time Management and Productivity:

- Todoist: A task management app that helps you stay organized and prioritize your to-do list.

- RescueTime: A time tracking and productivity tool that provides insights into how you spend your time and helps you optimize productivity.

- Forest: An app that uses gamification to encourage focus and discourage distractions by planting virtual trees during work sessions.

- Pomodoro Technique Apps: Apps like Focus Keeper or

Tomato Timer help implement the Pomodoro Technique, a time management method that uses timed work intervals and breaks to enhance productivity.

3. Travel Planning and Booking:

- Skyscanner: A flight search engine that compares prices across various airlines to help you find the best deals.

- Airbnb: A popular platform for finding accommodation, including apartments, houses, and unique stays in different destinations.

- Google Maps: A reliable navigation app that provides directions, maps, and information about local businesses and attractions.

- TripIt: A travel organizer app that consolidates all your travel plans, including flights, accommodations, and activities, in one place.

4. Language and Cultural Support:

- Duolingo: A language-learning app that offers interactive lessons in various languages to help you communicate better with locals.

- Google Translate: A versatile translation app that supports text, voice, and image translations for better communication in foreign languages.

- Culture Trip: A travel and cultural app that offers local guides, articles, and recommendations to help you immerse yourself in the local culture and experience hidden gems.

5. Financial Management:

- Xero or QuickBooks: Accounting software that helps you track expenses, create invoices, and manage your finances while on the go.

- Revolut or TransferWise: Digital banking apps that offer multi-currency accounts, low foreign exchange fees, and convenient money transfers.

Remember to explore these tools and apps to find the ones that best suit your needs and enhance your digital nomad experience. Embrace the power of technology to streamline your work, stay connected, and make the most of your nomadic journey.

Here's a checklist to help you transition into the digital nomad lifestyle:

1. Self-Reflection and Decision Making:

- Assess your motivation and reasons for becoming a digital nomad.

- Research and understand the challenges and rewards of the lifestyle.

- Determine if your work or profession is suitable for remote work.

2. Financial Preparation:

- Evaluate your current financial situation and create a budget.

- Save an emergency fund to cover unexpected expenses.

- Plan for health insurance and consider travel insurance options.

- Set up a system for managing finances while abroad (e.g., online banking, digital payment platforms).

3. Remote Work Setup:

- Ensure you have reliable internet access in your intended destinations.

- Set up a dedicated workspace with the necessary equipment (laptop, charger, external hard drive, etc.).

- Familiarize yourself with collaboration tools and software required for your work.

4. Travel Planning and Logistics:

- Choose your initial destination(s) and research visa requirements.

- Plan your travel itinerary, considering factors like cost of living, safety, and internet availability.

- Book accommodation, flights, and any necessary transportation in advance.

- Pack essential items, including travel adapters, portable chargers, and any specific work-related equipment.

5. Communication and Connectivity:

- Set up a reliable communication system (e.g., mobile plan, VoIP service) for staying in touch with clients, colleagues, and loved ones.

- Install essential communication apps like Slack, Zoom, and messaging platforms.

6. Health and Well-being:

- Research healthcare options and consider travel insurance that covers medical emergencies.

- Create a routine for exercise, healthy eating, and self-care while on the road.

- Ensure you have access to necessary medications and medical records.

7. Legal and Administrative Matters:

- Notify relevant authorities (e.g., tax office, insurance providers) about your change in status and address.

- Set up mail forwarding or utilize digital mail services.

- Familiarize yourself with local laws and customs in the destinations you plan to visit.

- Keep copies of important documents (e.g., passport, visas, health insurance) in a secure digital format.

8. Networking and Community:

- Join digital nomad forums, Facebook groups, or attend meetups to connect with like-minded individuals.

- Seek out co-working spaces or co-living communities to meet fellow nomads.

9. Mindset and Flexibility:

- Embrace the mindset of adaptability and flexibility to navigate uncertainties and challenges.

- Stay open to new experiences, cultures, and perspectives.

10. Enjoy the Journey:

- Embrace the adventure and make the most of your digital nomad lifestyle.

- Stay curious, explore new destinations, and find a healthy work-life balance.

Remember, this checklist is a starting point, and your journey as a digital nomad will be unique. Tailor it to your specific circumstances and needs, and don't forget to enjoy the freedom and opportunities that come with this remarkable lifestyle. Safe travels and may your digital nomad adventure be filled with joy, growth, and incredible experiences!

JANE-ANN KOCI

UNTITLED

ABOUT THE AUTHOR

Jane-Ann Koci

About the Author:

Jane-Ann Koci is a captivating storyteller, a free spirit with a Gypsy heritage, and a seasoned digital nomad. Her deep connection to the great outdoors and her innate wanderlust have fueled her extraordinary journey as she embraces a life of freedom, adventure, and self-discovery.

Jane-Ann's path to becoming a digital nomad was shaped by her experiences in human rights and social housing roles. Through partnerships and conferences across Europe, she discovered the transformative power of living and working in different places, sparking a fire within her to create a life aligned with her passions and desires.

With a background in advocacy and a relentless pursuit of justice, Jane-Ann carries the wisdom of embracing diversity, breaking free from limitations, and empowering others to embrace their own nomadic dreams. Her unique perspective as a Gypsy by heritage adds depth and richness to her storytelling, allowing readers to experience the world through her eyes and gain valuable insights into cultural immersion and understanding.

Jane-Ann's journey has taken her from the picturesque landscapes of Albania to the enchanting shores of Tunisia, and beyond. As a digital nomad, she has harnessed her skills and passions, teaching English online, practicing tarot and astrology, and diversifying her income streams to create a life of abundance and purpose.

In "Wanderlust Unleashed: A Digital Nomad's Guide to Embracing Freedom and Adventure," Jane-Ann shares her knowledge, experiences, and practical advice to inspire and empower readers to embark on their own nomadic journeys. Her words resonate with authenticity, offering guidance on financial preparation, remote work setup, travel logistics, work-life balance, and fostering a resilient mindset.

Through her storytelling prowess, Jane-Ann invites readers to imagine a life where work and travel intertwine seamlessly, where the world becomes their office and playground. She encourages individuals to embrace the unknown, dissolve the limitations, and create a life filled with adventure, self-discovery, and the pursuit of their passions.

Jane-Ann's genuine love for writing and storytelling shines through her work, captivating readers with her positive tone and empowering message. As an author, digital nomad, and advocate for freedom and diversity, she seeks to inspire others to break free from conventional norms and embark on a life-changing adventure that leads to personal and professional fulfillment.

Join Jane-Ann Koci on this remarkable journey, and let her be your guiding light as you embrace the digital nomad lifestyle. Prepare to unlock the potential within you, explore the world on your own terms, and create a life of freedom, adventure, and boundless possibilities.

Printed in Great Britain
by Amazon